This book is first of all dedicated
as a witness to Jesus Christ
and for His Honor and Glory.

Second of all it is dedicated in
loving memory to Jane Kranich
wonderful wife, mother,
grandmother, friend and poet!

Jesus Loves Us All

Poems about God and Jane's Relationship With Him
By Jane Kranich

Layout and Photography
By Bob Kranich

Edited by Joanne Kranich

Copyright 2015 by Jane Kranich
All rights reserved. No part of this book may be reproduced
in any form or by any means
without permission in writing from Bob or Joanne Kranich.

Book design by Bob Kranich

Self-Published by:
Bob & Joanne Kranich
White Post, Va.

Printed in the United States of America

Publisher's Cataloging-in-Publication-Data

Kranich, Jane.
Jesus loves us all : poems about God and Jane's relationship
with him / by Jane Kranich ;
layout and photography by Bob Kranich ; edited by Joanne Kranich.
p. cm.
ISBN 978-0-9716515-8-6

1. Christian poetry, American. I. Kranich, Bob. II. Kranich, Joanne. III. Title.

PS3561.R262 G64 2015
813.6—dc23
2015911525

First Paperback Edition

This book is dedicated to:
God

This book is first of all dedicated
as a witness to Jesus Christ
and for His Honor and Glory.

Second of all it is dedicated in
loving memory to Jane Kranich
wonderful wife, mother,
grandmother, friend and poet!

Table of Contents

Acknowledgements ix

Introduction xi

JESUS LOVES ME 1

NATURE CALLS... 3

HOPING FOR THE BEST 5

COUNT YOUR BLESSINGS 7

MY LAST WISHES.. 9

A PHONE CALL FROM GOD 11

LETTER TO GOD... 13

HEAVEN ON EARTH 15

DAY OF MEANING... 17

RETREAT IN THE MOUNTAINS......................... 19

A WELCOME VISITOR....................................... 21

THANK YOU LORD 23

NO ANSWER UP THERE................................... 25

SURPRISES ALL OVER THE PLACE 27

I WILL NEVER FORGET HIM 29

LORD'S DAY.. 31

ONLY GOD KNOWS	33
UNTIL WE MEET AGAIN	35
MY ALMOST VISIT TO HEAVEN	37
LEARNING HOW TO PRAY	39
PROMISE TO GOD	41
I'M THE LUCKY ONE	43
MY HEAVENLY DREAM	45
UNITED WE STAND	47
MY WONDERFUL CHILDREN	49
FEELING OF PEACE	51
THE LINE TO GOD WAS OPEN	53
CAN'T PLEASE EVERYONE	55
VISION IN GLASS	57
AGE DOESN'T MEAN A THING	59
OUR LADY OF CLEARWATER	62

Acknowledgements

In the writing of this book, <u>Jesus Loves Us All,</u> I first would like to give credit to God for giving me the creative ability to write poems. Writing poetry has been one of my best friends.

I thank my children for encouraging me to write all these years. It has been so helpful that every year faithfully Denise has compiled each years' poems into a small booklet for me to give as Christmas presents. Bob has selected these particular God poems for me from all of those books. He and his wife Joanne have worked together to put this book out especially for my 90th birthday. I thank all of them.

Again I thank each of my children Bob, Dave, Jackie and Denise for their love and support.

Jane Kranich

Introduction

I will be 90 years young when this book of poems is released. I think it's appropriate that it is about my relationship with God.

Truly my children have been my joy and hope especially since my husband's death – my best friend Al in 1999. Bob, Dave, Jackie and Denise are my treasures – each bringing into my life their own unique personalities and gifts.

But I also know that God has been with me in many special ways throughout all these years. In lonely moments and in happy moments – He is there. He has surprised me also. Whether through a vision in a bank window or through a stranger in a store – I know He is watching over me. I hope this book can be my "thank you" to God for His care and provision. It is also a "thank you" to Him for my 4 children, my grandchildren now and to come, and every family member and friend who brings me love and support.

I pray this book blesses you as much as it has blessed me to see it in its making.

Jane Kranich

JESUS LOVES ME

I was shopping in a grocery store, when a lady came by,
Put her arm around me, it was quite a surprise.
She said, "Jesus is watching you, and He loves you a lot."
He told me to tell you, that you will not be forgot.

She said that He wanted me to give you this-
      a twenty dollar bill,
Buy yourself something, that will give you a thrill.
I turned around, and the lady was nowhere to be found.
I thought about what she had said, and was dumbfound.

But I felt very special, and went on with my day,
after what happened, what can I say?

NATURE CALLS

I like to write about nature, the ocean, the clouds, and the trees,
One could go on forever with just the beauty of the leaves.
I watch the clouds at daylight or just before a storm,
Or at night with the stars twinkling, it's a joy to have been born.

I can't explain the feelings, they get stronger every day,
Maybe now that I am older, I appreciate the rays of the sun,
The moon, the seasons, I love each and every one.

Nature is here for one and all,
So listen and enjoy the calls.

HOPING FOR THE BEST

Being a Mom has been special to me,
Little ones sitting on top of my knee.
Dirty faces and tousled hair,
There is nothing on earth that can compare.

To know that they are yours forever,
Sent straight down to you from heaven.
Little angels so sweet and frail,
All depending on you to care.

So as they grow and look your way,
You have done your duty every day.
To see that they know wrong from right,
And hope everything would turn out right.

I'm the Mom and I passed the test,
And now we can only hope for the best.

COUNT YOUR BLESSINGS

It's rainy, dark, and dreary out,
The whole world is upside down.
I can't find a reason to shout,
Or why I should get rid of this frown.
I keep finding fault with everything,
(My life, my loved ones, my friends.)

When I think it can't get any worse,
And I'm at my deepest end.
A voice pops into my head,
"Count your blessings, friend."
Then I think how blessed I am,
And I am ashamed of my thoughts.
I should be on my knees and pray,
That I am not the one caught.

So now it's light and cheery out,
And the world is smiling at me.
I count my blessings every day,
And life is full of glee.

MY LAST WISHES

As I head into my last remaining years,
I tend to reminisce, and it brings a few tears.
It also brings a few wishes, along the way,
For my last remaining days.
Please grant me a longer life for one,
I don't want to leave until my work is done.
I want my children to have the best,
That life will give them, nothing less.
I want everyone to get along…
Nice to one another, and join in song.
Think of this as your very last day,
Join hands, and kneel, and pray.

A PHONE CALL FROM GOD

I had a call from God today,
A phone call, what can I say.
I was so shaken, I had to sit down,
His voice was so normal, I was dumbfound.
He said, "And how are you today?"
He didn't sound that far away,
I was wondering why is God calling me,
And I started shaking in my knees.
I said, "But God, how do I know it's really You?"
And He said, "Hang up the phone,
      and I'll still come through."
I did as He said, and He came through loud and clear,
He said, "I'll talk to you later and have no fear.
Tell everyone I love them all,
And soon will be giving them a call."

LETTER TO GOD

I'm writing a letter to God today,
I have lots of things I want to say.
I need to ask Him, in a nice way,
How much longer do we have to pay,
For other people's wicked ways?

What do we do? Where do we go?
They are crowding us out in the cold.
I don't want to yell and shout,
Just ask God, what it's all about?

So God, You need to take a stand,
And come visit Your long lost land.

HEAVEN ON EARTH

The pitter patter of little feet running down the hall,
Then happy voices shouting, "Mommy, we heard you call."
Suddenly sweet little arms smothering you with love,
And you take the time to say thank you to the Lord above.
Heaven on earth is here, and there is nothing sweeter,
Than little children to bring us happy tears.
God Bless Us.

DAY OF MEANING

"God" made this perfect day today,
    And nothing can go wrong.
The grass is greener, the sky is bluer,
    And the birds are singing our song.

I have never seen a prettier day,
    I don't know what it is.
All I know is I'm in love,
    And nothing can go amiss.

I'm in love with all the seconds and minutes,
    And hours of the day.
And let's not forget,
    The wonderful sun's rays.

I have never been so happy,
    And I thank the good Lord for my life.
My days are filled with all the ways
    For me to see the light.

RETREAT IN THE MOUNTAINS

I went to a church retreat in the mountains,
    My children took me there.
The leaves were changing, beautiful colors,
    And there was a chill in the air.
We stayed in a quaint little house set among the greens,
    The quiet was all around us, and it was so serene.
We felt near to God, and we know He was nearby,
    Watching us from the beautiful blue sky.
I met so many nice people that took me in their fold,
    I felt so loved and wanted, they treated me like gold.
Next Fall they will have the retreat again,
    and I would like to be there,
    A weekend at the mountains for me is very rare.
So I'm looking forward to going again. under that beautiful sky,
    So until we meet again, I will say my good byes.

A WELCOME VISITOR

I saw an angel this morning,
    She came to visit me.
I didn't know what this visit meant,
    But it was a wonderful sight to see.
I've had some problems in my life,
    And I have been under a lot of stress.
So when I saw this angel I thought,
    "This is some kind of a test."
She stayed with me and we talked and talked,
    And suddenly I felt so free.
The problems I thought were so big,
    Turned out to be mostly imagined by me.
This angel turned my life around,
    And I want to thank her for her time.
But she disappeared, and I know she left happy,
    Because she knows that I'm now fine.

THANK YOU LORD

I had a vision this morning – about a friend of mine,
She was coming to visit, and I know this vision was a sign.

I called her and told her to be careful on the road,
And to take a different route than she had planned,
       Because this route was on overload.

She said, "Thanks I will take extra care
I will take a different route,
So I can be prepared."

She arrived safe and sound,
And later we heard on TV,
       That the road she was going to take,
       Was now a battleground.

There were several accidents and people had died.
She looked at me awe and started to cry,
And said, "How did you know?"
I said, "I have a little ESP from a long time ago."
I hope it never leaves me,
This time it saved my friend from a catastrophe.

NO ANSWER UP THERE

I'm calling Heaven,
      Will someone please answer up there?
I've been calling and calling,
      But there is something wrong somewhere.

The phone keeps ringing and ringing,
      But no one answers my calls.
I need to get through,
      Before I start climbing the walls.

I need to talk to someone,
      It's very important to me.
My loved one died last night,
      So you see.
Why I have to get in touch with Heaven,
      And talk to my Loved One once more.
Tell him how much I love him,
      Before they close the doors.

So, please, will someone in heaven,
      Please answer my call,
      Please answer my call.

SURPRISES ALL OVER THE PLACE

My children bought me a new washing machine,
    My old one leaked so bad.
I also got a new fridge and a new sofa,
    Made me feel so glad.
Surprises all over the place, I don't know what to do.
    Every time I turned around there was something, new.
I felt so proud and lucky to be so loved,
    That I took time out to thank the good Lord above.

Jesus Loves Us All　　28

I WILL NEVER FORGET HIM

My Al died five years ago, and
    I still have most of his things to show.
I don't want to ever forget him,
    He was my very best friend.
Some people told me,
    I should store his things.
So I wouldn't feel sad, but
    Just seeing his things round makes me feel glad.
I still have his old motorcycle helmet,
    He use to wear.
When we took those motorcycle rides,
    All around the countryside.
I could go on and on,
    As the memories keep rolling in,
And I'm going to keep them all inside me,
    through thick and thin.

LORD'S DAY`

I stayed home all day today,
.   Watched a couple movies to help pass the time away.
Then I watched an hour of religion too,
    It's Sunday, and the Lord's Day to pay tribute to.

I like the program called Gaithers' Hour,
    Lots of singing to devour.
After the evening is done,
    Time to say good night to everyone.
It's a day well spent,
    And I'm so content.
I feel good inside,
    And filled with pride.

ONLY GOD KNOWS

God must have a reason to let me live this long,
    Whatever it is, I'm trying to be strong.
I'm a good person, trying my best,
    Because I know one of these days, I will be His guest.
So many of my friends and relatives too,
    Are in His home looking down from the blue.
So whatever plan God has for me,
    I will gladly agree.

UNTIL WE MEET AGAIN

I wanted to stay a little longer,
But God said the time is here.
So I just dropped what I was doing,
Because I knew it was for real.

I'm going home,
My visit here is done.
I've had a wonderful life,
And I'm going to miss everyone.

But my real home is Heaven,
And we are only on earth for a while.
So until we meet again,
Keep that wonderful smile.

MY ALMOST VISIT TO HEAVEN

I almost died 63 years ago,
      I remember floating on a little mat above,
          Looking down below.
I could see what was happening with doctors
      Running here and there,
         With oxygen tanks and other hospital wares.

The doctor said later he almost lost us both,
      My baby son and I came that close.
But something kept us fighting,
      And we made it through.
This happened 63 years ago and still holds true.

LEARNING HOW TO PRAY

Put your hands together and say a prayer,
It won't hurt, only help you care.
So many things you can ask God to bless,
You will only feel more love, not less.
I know you're lost and a little shy,
But if you follow my lead, you won't ask why.
You will know in a second, it's the right thing to do,
We will pray for others, then pray for you.

PROMISE TO GOD

I watched you sleep,
    My precious baby of a few hours old.
Thinking of the miracle of birth,
    So deep it can never be told.
How this perfect angel,
Who arrived so loving and so dear.
Wondering what the fuss was about,
    And letting everyone around that could hear.
This beautiful child is mine,
    Forever to have and hold.
Worth all to me,
    Than all of anyone's gold.
I'm going to love you forever,
    And dream of your future to be.
I'm making my promise to God,
    And you just wait and see.

I'M THE LUCKY ONE

I have to tell you how precious you are to me,
    If I can find the words to have you believe.
You're the moon, stars and the sun all wrapped up together,
    No matter what kind of weather.

I love you more than words can say,
    You are the center of my thoughts through the day.
I'm the luckiest person in the world today,
    Because I have you to think about in every way.

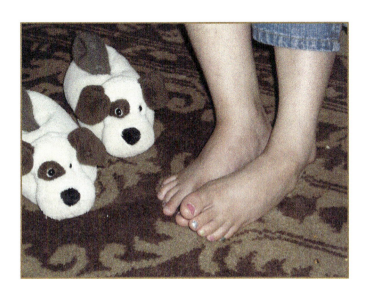

MY HEAVENLY DREAM

The other night when I was watching TV,
    I looked outside, and Jesus was watching me.
He was near the trees, right outside my door,
    "I blinked" a few times, then said, "Oh, my Lord."

He looked older than I imagined Him to be,
    But I would know Him anywhere,
And it was a wonderful sight to see.

It was only His face that I could see,
    As He looked around from the trees.
It was a beautiful picture, and He didn't stay long,
    But I felt so honored, I wanted to sing a song.

I don't know if anyone else saw Him, (I didn't ask around,)
    I didn't want to make a sound.
I just felt so honored that He was looking at me,
    (Nodding and smiling), that's all I could see.

Maybe it's a sign from above,
    That Jesus is showing his love.
And when you least expect it, you may also see,
    Jesus smiling at you from your tree.

UNITED WE STAND

God Bless America,
      The flags are everywhere.
It gives one such a feeling of peace,
      To know everyone cares.

Everywhere you go, in any kind of weather,
      This is America, they chant,
And we unite together.

God Bless America
      No one will ever get us down.
We love our country and will do our best,
      To keep America sound.

MY WONDERFUL CHILDREN

My children are so wonderful ,
        I can't imagine my life alone.
When they were little,
        They were such a delight.
And now they are older,
        They call me on the phone.

How are you doing Mom?
        Are you OK?
How did you sleep last night?
        And what are you doing today?

We are sending you some money,
        Buy yourself something nice.
Something you always wanted,
        But was afraid of the price.

We are coming over Sunday,
        Bringing your grandchildren along.
They are all excited because they are going,
        To sing you a special song.

We all love you Mom,
        And you are part of us.
Take care of yourself,
        You know we love to fuss.

I couldn't do without my children,
        They are my life.
I lay awake sometimes at night.
And thank the Lord,
For making my days so bright.

FEELING OF PEACE

I felt a hand on my shoulder today,
    It startled me in every way.

No one was in the room, but me
    And there was no one else to see.
I don't know who it was or what it could be,
    But a wonderful sense of peace came over me.

I have been under a lot of stress,
    And I think someone was trying their best.
To let me know, I'm going to be fine,
    I'm not alone and just give myself time.

I believe in angels and Heaven above,
    And I believe in the good Lord's love.
So it gave me a wonderful feeling inside,
    To suddenly feel so alive.

THE LINE TO GOD WAS OPEN

I was sitting outside, looking up at the blue,
When all of a sudden, I felt a connection to You.

The line was open (all the way),
and I knew I should talk to You,
But I didn't know what to say.

I couldn't imagine being able to talk to You,
I know how many people are trying to get through.

So I stuttered and stammered and said,
"Hi God I'm doing OK
        and I have lots of things I would like to say."
But I know other people need You more, so I will just say,
"I love you God" and then You can close the door.

Now that I know, I can talk to You, I will be back,
        And look up at the blue,
And hope I can find the line open again.
        So when ever I need to, I can talk to You.

CAN'T PLEASE EVERYONE

Some people say there are not enough hours in the day,
    To do all the things they have to do,
And get enough sleep to pull them through.

Other people say the days are too long,
    And the hours in the day are all wrong.

Can't please everyone, but God made the days,
    And it is up to you to be sad or gay.
So try to enjoy the time God gave you,
    And His love will pull you through.

VISION IN GLASS

A vision in glass is what they see,
They come in crowds of one, two and three.
Not just the vision-it's a spiritual sight,
Everyone comes to see the light.

It's the Virgin Mary,
As you can see.
Surrounded by colors,
As bright as can be.

Whatever the reason,
She's here to stay.
To bring joy to people,
Who kneel down to pray.

* (See page 62 for story)

Jesus Loves Us All

AGE DOESN'T MEAN A THING

I may be going on 90,
        But I don't think I'm old.
All my thoughts are young at heart,
        Everybody tells me so.

I like to take a walk at night,
        Under the stars and moon so bright.
I like to giggle at movie shows,
        and wear teeny bopper clothes.

They always say you're as old as you feel,
        Sometimes I'm 21.
I have to pinch myself sometimes,
        I'm having so much fun!

I have no plans to change my ways!
        I'm enjoying my last remaining days!

Our Lady of Clearwater

It was a sunny day in 1996 on Hwy 19 in Clearwater, Florida. A lady parked her car in her bank parking lot and went inside. After completing her financial transactions, she went out to the parking lot to her car. As she was opening the car door, she glanced up at the bank. There formed on nine of the large panels of glass was the image of the Virgin Mary.

She hurriedly went back into the bank and told one of the bank officers, "The Virgin Mary is on your outside windows", they went outside to look. The newspapers and TV station were called, and the story was on the evening news and in the newspapers the next day.

Hundreds, then thousands of people came to look. The streets and parking lot got clogged with people and cars! The Clearwater police had to direct traffic and close some streets. Over the weeks following the bank had a difficult time conducting their business. The end result was that a Catholic religious group came down from Ohio to preserve the image. Through negotiations, the Shepherds of Christ Ministries presently is purchasing the building. The bank has since moved.

Today, nuns in white habits move about taking care of the religious services and the gift shop. They are paying for the building with donations. People still come to see and pray at the image. Not in the thousands of curiosity seekers, but the religious few who feel led to visit.

In 2004 a tragic incident took place. A young man shot out the three top panes of glass with a powerful sling shot.

He was soon apprehended, but the religious order, in the spirit of forgiveness, did not press charges. Some time later after this incident another miracle happened. The face of a man can be seen in the bosom of the Virgin Mary's image. (Jesus) (see on page 24)

You may visit the Our Lady of Clearwater at:

21649 US 19
Clearwater, Florida

*If you liked this book by Jane Kranich
You may be interested in these books by Jane.
Check out her web site at* www.janekranich.com

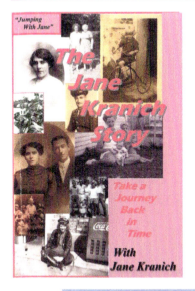

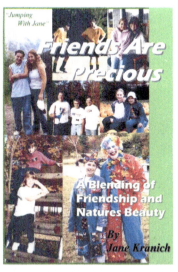

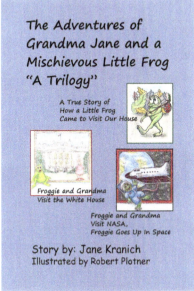

CPSIA information can be obtained at www.ICGtesting.com
Printed in the USA
BVOW11s0126051015
420486BV00002B/2/P